MORE OF
WHO SAID THAT?

MORE OF
WHO SAID THAT?

Quotations and biographies
of famous people

Selected and compiled by
RENIE GEE

David & Charles
Newton Abbot   London   North Pomfret (Vt)

British Library Cataloguing in Publication Data

More of who said that?
   1. Quotations, English
   2. Biography
   I. Gee, Renie
   920'.02   PN6081

   ISBN 0–7153–8275–6

Typeset by
Northern Phototypesetting Co, Bolton
and printed in Great Britain
by A. Wheaton & Co, Exeter
for David & Charles (Publishers) Limited
Brunel House, Newton Abbot, Devon

Published in the United States of America
by David & Charles Inc, North Pomfret,
Vermont 05053 USA

INTRODUCTION

When *Who Said That?* was published, it raised many questions. Why, people asked, did you not include some of the best pieces by Dorothy Parker, by Thomas Hardy, or W. H. Davies the Supertramp? The answer, of course, was space. To produce a book including everyone's favourite quotation would make it merely another reference book, and an expensive one too.

The *Who Said That?* books are 'fun books' − books aimed at giving the reader pleasure, books which can be picked up in an idle moment and looked through with interest and amusement. If you find your favourite quotation here, that surely is added delight.

In this second book I have tried to include all my friends' suggestions. You will find, as requested, Dorothy Parker, Thomas Hardy, W. H. Davies and many more, including a number of French authors to please a French friend, besides, of course, a selection from the tried and true pieces we all learnt at school.

I have much enjoyed compiling this second book in the series. I hope you enjoy it too.

RENIE GEE

To
dear Christine, who does so much,
and to Alice, Ann and Alison, with love

Aesop

Beware lest you lose the substance by grasping at the shadow.

Fables

The gods help them that help themselves.

Fables

It is not only fine feathers that make fine birds.

Fables

Don't count your chickens before they are hatched.

Fables

Aesop (c550BC), a fabulist of antiquity, is said by Herodotus to have lived in the reign of Amasis of Egypt. Originally a slave, he is represented in later art as deformed, but he received his freedom and travelled as far afield as Greece. .

Henry Aldrich

If all be true that I do think,
There are five reasons we should drink;
Good wine – a friend – or being dry –
Or lest we should be by and by –
Or any other reason why.

Reasons for Drinking

Henry Aldrich (1647-1710) was an English scholar who became dean of Christ Church, Oxford, in 1689 and remained in office until his death. He designed the Peckwater Quadrangle at Christ Church, adapted anthems and church music, and wrote some humorous verse.

Matthew Arnold

The sea is calm tonight.
The tide is full, the moon lies fair
Upon the Straits.

Dover Beach

Runs it not here, the track by Childsworth Farm,
Past the high wood, to where the elm-tree crowns
The hill behind whose ridge the sunset flames?

Thyrsis

Once I knew each field, each flower, each stick,
And with the country-folk acquaintance made –

Thyrsis

Matthew Arnold (1822-88), the British poet and son of the famous Doctor Arnold, headmaster of Rugby School, was elected professor of poetry at Oxford. He wrote a classical tragedy (*Merope*) and *New Poems*, and these were followed by *Essays in Criticism*, some studies in education, *Literature and Dogma* and *Culture and Anarchy*.

Pierre Balmain

The trick of wearing mink is to look as though you are wearing a cloth coat. The trick of wearing a cloth coat is to look as though you are wearing mink.

Newspaper report

Pierre Alexandre Balmain (1914-) was educated at the Lyćee de Chambéry and Ecole des Beaux-Arts, Paris. He was a dress designer with Molyneux and then with Lucien Lelong, and became established as a couturier in 1946.

Honoré de Balzac

Love is perhaps but gratitude for pleasure.

A good husband is never the first to go to sleep at night or the last to awake in the morning.

Children! You bring them into the world, and they drive you out of it.

The man who can govern a woman can govern a nation.

Laws are spider webs that catch little flies, but cannot hold big ones.

Honoré de Balzac (1799-1850) was the son of the director of the City Hospital at Tours. After studying law he turned to literature, but at first with little success. From 1829 onwards he wrote many novels which were to become famous.

J. M. Barrie

It's a sort of bloom on a woman. If you have it [charm] you don't need to have anything else.
What Every Woman Knows

His lordship may compel us to be equal upstairs, but there will never be equality in the servants' hall.
The Admirable Crichton

Sir James Matthew Barrie (1860-1937), the Scottish novelist and dramatist, became editorial writer for the Nottingham Journal in 1883, but turning to fiction he had great success, particularly with *Peter Pan*, *Mary Rose* and *Dear Brutus*.

Max Beerbohm

You cannot make a man by standing a sheep on its legs. But by standing a flock of sheep in that position you can make a crowd of men.

Sir Max Beerbohm (1872-1956) was an English writer who was the half-brother of the actor-manager Sir Herbert Beerbohm-Tree. He contributed to *The Yellow Book of Essays* and succeeded Shaw as dramatic critic to the *Saturday Review*. He was knighted in 1939.

Hilaire Belloc

I'm tired of Love: I'm still more tired of Rhyme.
But Money gives me pleasure all the time.
Epigrams

The Llama is a woolly sort of fleecy hairy goat,
With an indolent expression and an undulating throat.
More Beasts for Worse Children

9

I will hold my house in the high wood
Within a walk of the sea,
And the men that were boys when I was a boy
Shall sit and drink with me.

The South Country

Joseph Hilaire Pierre Belloc (1870-1953) was the son of a French barrister and an English mother. He founded the *Eye-Witness* in collaboration with Cecil Chesterton, with whom he also wrote a political work entitled *The Party System*. He also worked with G. K. Chesterton, and his literary versatility is shown by his nonsense verse, his historical studies of Danton, Robespierre and James II, his *History of England*, and various satires.

Robert Benchley

I do most of my work sitting down; that's where I shine.

Robert Benchley (1889-1945), the American humorist, was born at Worcester, Mass, went to New York as a journalist and became drama editor of the *New Yorker*. His books *Of All Things* and *Benchley Beside Himself* demonstrate his fine ability to extract humour from daily life.

Josh Billings

Thrice is he armed that hath his quarrel just
But four times he who gets his blow in fust.

Josh Billings, his Sayings

Josh Billings (1818-85) was the pseudonym of Henry Wheeler Shaw, an American humorous writer. His popular work *Josh Billings, His Sayings* depended for its humour on mis-spellings, puns, and malapropisms.

Laurence Binyon

They shall not grow old, as we that are left grow old;
Age shall not weary them, nor the years condemn.
At the going down of the sun, and in the morning,
We will remember them.

For the Fallen

Laurence Binyon (1869-1943) was born at Lancaster, the son of a clergyman, and became Keeper of prints and drawings at the British Museum. He published some studies of English and Eastern art, but is best remembered for his fine ode *For the Fallen*, which was written in 1914.

William Blake

Tyger! Tyger! burning bright
In the forests of the night,
What immortal hand or eye
Could frame thy fearful symmetry?

Songs of Experience: The Tyger

Bring me my bow of burning gold!
Bring me my arrows of desire!
Bring me my spear! O clouds, unfold!
Bring me my chariot of fire.

I will not cease from mental fight,
Nor shall my sword sleep in my hand,
Till we have built Jerusalem
In England's green and pleasant land.

Milton, preface

To see a World in a Grain of Sand,
And a Heaven in a Wild Flower —
Hold Infinity in the palm of your hand,
And Eternity in an hour.

Auguries of Innocence

William Blake (1757-1827) was apprenticed to an engraver and studied at the Academy under Reynolds. He engraved the illustrations for his *Book of Thel*, *Marriage of Heaven and Hell* and *Song of Los*, but after the failure of an exhibition in 1809 he retired from engraving. His works include *Milton*, *Jerusalem* and the fragmentary *Everlasting Gospel*.

Robert Browning

Oh, to be in England
Now that April's there . . .

Home-thoughts, from Abroad

Hamelin Town's in Brunswick,
By famous Hanover city;
The river Weser, deep and wide,
Washes its walls on the southern side.

The Pied Piper of Hamelin

Into the street the Piper stept,
Smiling first a little smile,
As if he knew what magic slept
In his quiet pipe the while . . .

The Pied Piper of Hamelin

And the mutterings grew to a grumbling,
And the grumbling grew to a mighty rumbling;
And out of the houses the rats came tumbling . . .

The Pied Piper of Hamelin

From street to street he piped, advancing,
And step by step they followed, dancing.

The Pied Piper of Hamelin

Robert Browning (1812-89), born at Camberwell, was the son of a clerk in the Bank of England. Educated at a private school and at home, he travelled a great deal in Europe. Devoting his whole life to poetry, he published his first piece *Pauline* in 1833, but in 1835 his *Paracelsus* attracted the friendly notice of Carlyle, Wordsworth, and other men of letters. He married Elizabeth Barrett and lived with her in Italy, but when she died he returned to London and published many more pieces of poetry.

George Burns

My secret for longevity? Drinking martinis, smoking cigars.

George Burns (1898-) first made his name in Vaudeville as a dancer. Then he teamed up with Gracie Allen, and together they toured the USA and Europe, making their radio debut with the BBC. In 1976 he received an Academy Award for Best Supporting Actor in the film *The Sunshine Boys*.

Samuel Butler

Brigands demand your money or your life; women require both.

Samuel Butler (1612-80), the English satirical poet, was for a time page to the Countess of Kent, and later became steward of Ludlow Castle. He was the author of *Hudibras*, a much-quoted mock-heroic poem satirising the hypocrisy, churlishness, greed, pride and casuistry of the Presbyterians and Independents.

Thomas Carlyle

The block of granite which was an obstacle in the pathway of the weak, became a stepping-stone in the pathway of the strong.

The three great elements of modern civilization, Gunpowder, Printing, and the Protestant Religion.
Critical and Miscellaneous Essays

Happy the people whose annals are blank in history books!
Frederick the Great, Bk XVI

No great man lives in vain. The history of the world is but the biography of great men.
Heroes and Hero Worship

Thomas Carlyle (1795-1881) was a Scottish author who studied for the Presbyterian ministry but later gave up the Church and combined study of the law with miscellaneous literary work. He established his reputation with *The French Revolution*, which is said to be still unrivalled in its vividness of narration.

Lewis Carroll

'What is the use of a book', thought Alice, 'without pictures or conversations?'
Alice's Adventures in Wonderland

Take care of the sense, and the sounds will take care of themselves.
Alice's Adventures in Wonderland

13

'Reeling and Writhing, of course, to begin with,' the Mock Turtle replied; 'and then the different branches of Arithmetic — Ambition, Distraction, Uglification, and Derision.'

Alice's Adventures in Wonderland

'Twas brillig and the slithy toves
Did gyre and gimble in the wabe.
All mincing were the borogoves
And the nome raths outgrabe.

Through the Looking-Glass:
Jabberwocky

Curtsey while you're thinking what to say. It saves time.

Through the Looking-Glass

The rule is, jam to-morrow and jam yesterday — but never jam to-day.

Through the Looking-Glass

He would answer to 'Hi!' or to any loud cry,
Such as 'Fry me!' or 'Fritter my wig!'
To 'What-you-may-call-um!' or 'What-was-his-name!'
But especially 'Thing-um-a-jig!'

The Hunting of the Snark

Lewis Carroll (1839-98) was the pseudonym of Charles Lutwidge Dodgson, a mathematician and writer of children's books. He became a lecturer in mathematics at Oxford and published books on the subject, but became famous for *Alice's Adventures in Wonderland*. This grew out of a story told by Dodgson to amuse three little girls, including the original Alice — Alice Liddell, daughter of the dean of Christ Church. Later he published *Through the Looking Glass* and *The Hunting of the Snark*.

Barbara Cartland

I'll wager you that in ten years it will be fashionable again to be a virgin.

20.6.1976

There's no substitute for moonlight and kissing.

11.9.1977

Barbara Cartland (1901-) is a very popular writer. She published her first novel at the age of twenty-one, which ran into five editions. Since then she has written hundreds of romantic novels as well as biographies, cookery books, plays, and some verse, and has designed and organised many pageants in aid of charity. She has also made frequent radio and television appearances.

Nicholas Chamfort

A day is wasted without laughter.

The highest qualities often unfit a man for society. We don't take ingots with us to market, we take silver or small change.

Society is composed of two large classes; those who have more dinners than appetites, and those who have more appetite than dinners.

In great matters men try to show themselves to their best advantage; in small matters they show themselves as they are.

Sebastien Roch Nicholas Chamfort (1741-94) was a French writer and wit. At the outbreak of the Revolution he joined the Jacobins, took part in the storming of the Bastille, and bitterly attacked the National Convention. He mortally wounded himself when about to be arrested. He is best known for his *Maximes*, which was published posthumously, but he was also author of comedies, literary criticisms, letters, and verse.

Sir Winston Churchill

These two great organisations of the English-speaking democracies, the British Empire and the United States, will have to be somewhat mixed up together in some of their affairs ... I do not view the process with any misgivings. I could not stop it if I wished; no one can stop it. Like the Mississippi, it just keeps rolling along. Let it roll. Let it roll on full flood, inexorable, irresistible, benignant, to broader lands and better days.

Speech: House of Commons, 20.8.1940

Sir Winston Leonard Spencer Churchill (1874-1965) was a descendant of the great Duke of Marlborough. Churchill was born at Blenheim Palace, the elder son of Lord Randolph Churchill and his American wife, Jenny Jerome. During the Boer War he was war correspondent of the *Morning Post*, was taken prisoner, but made a dramatic escape.

Elected Conservative MP for Oldham in 1900, he disagreed with Chamberlain's tariff reform policy and joined the Liberals, later becoming President of the Board of Trade. As Minister of Munitions under Lloyd George, he had much to do with the development of the tank, and during the Second World War as Prime Minister he became famous for his rallying speeches.

As well as being a great war leader, Churchill was a distinguished writer. In 1953 he won the Nobel Prize for Literature.

John Clare

If life had a second edition, how I would correct the proofs.
Letter to a friend

John Clare (1793-1864), the poet, was born near Peterborough, the son of a farm labourer, and passed most of his days in poverty. He wrote *Poems Descriptive of Rural Life, The Village Minstrel* and *The Shepherd's Calendar*. He was given an annuity by the Duke of Exeter and other patrons but had to return to the land.

Arthur Hugh Clough

Do not adultery commit;
Advantage rarely comes of it.
The Latest Decalogue

Grace is given of God, but knowledge is bought in the market.
The Bothie of Tober-na-Vuolich

When daylight comes, comes in the light,
In front the sun climbs slow, how slowly,
But westward, look, the land is bright.
Say not the Struggle Naught Availeth

Arthur Hugh Clough (1819-61), the British poet, was born in Liverpool, the son of a rich cotton merchant, and was at Rugby under the famous Doctor Arnold. His poem *Say not the Struggle Naught Availeth* was made famous during the Second World War because it was quoted by Sir Winston Churchill in one of his war speeches.

S. T. Coleridge

Therefore all seasons shall be sweet to thee,
Whether the summer clothe the general earth
With greenness, or redbreast sit and sing
Betwixt the tufts of snow on the bare branch.

All Seasons Shall be Sweet

They stood aloof, the scars remaining,
Like cliffs which had been rent asunder . . .

Christabel

The Knight's bones are dust,
And his good sword rust –
His soul is with the saints, I trust.

The Knight's Tomb

Not the poem which we have *read*, but that to which we *return* with the greatest pleasure, possesses the genuine power, and claims the name of *essential poetry*.

Biographia Literaria

I wish our clever young poets would remember my homely definitions of prose and poetry; that is, prose = words in their best order; – poetry = the *best* words in the best order.

Table Talk

Samuel Taylor Coleridge (1772-1834), son of the vicar of Ottery St Mary, Devon, was educated at Christ's Hospital and Jesus College, Cambridge. He contributed verses to the *Morning Chronicle* and collaborated with Wordsworth in *Lyrical Ballads*, which contained his *Ancient Mariner*. In 1798 he visited Germany, where he became interested in German literature and philosophy. The best of his criticism is found in *Biographia Literaria* and *Table Talk*.

William Congreve

Music hath charms to soothe a savage breast,
To soften rocks, or bend a knotted oak.

The Mourning Bride

Heav'n has no rage, like love to hatred turn'd,
Nor Hell a fury like a woman scorn'd.

The Mourning Bride

Let us be very strange and well-bred: Let us be as strange
as if we had been married a great while, and as well-bred as
if we were not married at all.   *The Way of the World*

Defer not till to-morrow to be wise.
To-morrow's sun to thee may never rise.

Letter to Viscount Cobham

William Congreve (1670-1729) was born near Leeds, was a
friend of Swift at Trinity College, Dublin, and then
studied law in London. He won immediate success with his
first comedy *The Old Bachelor* and this was followed by
The Double Dealer, Love for Love and his tragedy *The
Mourning Bride*. His masterpiece *The Way of the World*
was at first regarded as a failure. Congreve is regarded by
many people as the most brilliant of the Restoration comic
dramatists.

William Cowper

How much a dunce that has been sent to roam
Excels a dunce that has been kept at home.

The Progress of Error

Pernicious weed! whose scent the fair annoys,
Unfriendly to society's chief joys,
Thy worst effect is banishing for hours
The sex whose presence civilizes ours.   *Conversation*

Twelve years have elapsed since I last took a view
Of my favourite field, and the bank where they [poplars]
grew;
And now in the grass behold they are laid,
And the tree is my seat that once lent me a shade.

The Poplar-Field

William Cowper (1731-1800) began his literary work with the hymns he wrote with the Reverend John Newton, but later Mrs Unwin persuaded him to write poetry, and a volume of poems appeared in 1782. Lady Austen told him the story of John Gilpin, which became the subject of one of his most popular poems, and she also persuaded him to write his greatest work *The Task*.

Oliver Cromwell

What shall we do with this bauble? There, take it away.

Of the Mace, when dismissing
Parliament, 20.4.1653

Mr. Lely, I desire you would use all your skill to paint my picture truly like me, and not flatter me at all; but remark all these roughnesses, pimples, warts, and everything as you see me, otherwise I will never pay a farthing for it.

Remark: Walpole's Anecdotes
of Painting

Oliver Cromwell (1599-1658) was born at Huntingdon, the son of a small landowner, and was educated at the local grammar school and at Cambridge. Active in the events leading to the Civil War, he raised a troop of horse and was engaged in the Battle of Edgehill. After that he raised more cavalry forces, which were chiefly responsible for the victory at Marston Moor. Cromwell was a member of the special commission which tried the King and condemned him to death, and later he assumed the title of Protector, with almost royal powers.

W. H. Davies

What is this life if, full of care,
We have no time to stand and stare?
No time to stand beneath the boughs
And stare as long as sheep or cows.

Leisure

Welcome to you, rich Autumn days,
Here comes the cold, leaf-picking wind,
When golden stocks are seen in fields –
All standing arm-in-arm entwined.

Rich Days

19

William Henry Davies (1871-1940), the British poet, went to America and for years lived the life of a hobo. He lost his right foot while 'riding the rods', and later returned to England and published his first volume of poems *Soul's Destroyer*. While living the life of a wandering pedlar he published more volumes of simple verse and the prose work *The Autobiography of a Supertramp*.

Sammy Davis Junior

I invented controversy, but not on purpose.

My own rules are very simple. Don't hurt nobody. Be nice to people.

Sammy Davis Junior (1925-) began his theatrical life by taking part in films, then made Vaudeville appearances with a trio. He became singer, dancer, impressionist and recorder of songs for various companies, and has written his autobiography, which he has called *Yes I Can*.

Charles Dickens

C-l-e-a-n, clean, verb active, to make bright, to scour. W-i-n, win, d-e-r, der, winder, or casement. When the boy knows this out of the book, he goes and does it.
Nicholas Nickleby, Mr. Squeers

Miss Bolo rose from the table considerably agitated, and went straight home, in a flood of tears and a sedan chair.
Pickwick Papers

Accidents will occur in the best-regulated families.
David Copperfield, Mr. Micawber

It's over, and can't be helped, and that's one consolation, as they always say in Turkey, ven they cuts the wrong man's head off.
Pickwick Papers, Sam Weller

Any man may be in good spirits and good temper when he's well dressed.
Martin Chuzzlewit, Mark Tapley

'It is', says Chadband, 'the rays of rays, the sun of suns, the moon of moons, the star of stars.'

Bleak House

It is a far, far better thing that I do, than I have ever done; it is a far, far better rest I go to, than I have ever known.

A Tale of Two Cities, Sidney Carton

Charles Dickens (1812-70), the son of a government clerk who was imprisoned in the Marshalsea prison for debt, used many of his own unhappy experiences in the books he wrote. Eventually he became parliamentary reporter for the *Morning Chronicle*, to which he contributed his *Sketches by Boz*. His *Pickwick Papers* were originally intended as an accompaniment to a series of sporting illustrations, but the adventures of Pickwick outgrew their setting and established Dickens' position as a writer.

Benjamin Disraeli

The question is this: is man an ape or an angel? Now I am on the side of the angels.

Speech, Oxford 25.11.1864

A University should be a place of light, of liberty, and of learning.

Speech in House of Commons, 11.3.1873

Benjamin Disraeli (1804-81), first Earl of Beaconsfield, was the eldest son of Isaac D'Israeli and received his literary training chiefly in his father's library. He published his first novel *Vivian Grey* in his twenty-second year. In 1837 he entered parliament as member for Maidstone, and became leader of a small group called The Young England Party. Their ideas are described in his novels *Coningsby and Tancredi*. In his last year as Prime Minister (1880) he published his novel *Endymion*.

Henry Austin Dobson

The ladies of St. James's!
They're painted to the eyes,
Their white it stays for ever,
Their red it never dies.

The Ladies of St. James's

But Phyllida, my Phyllida!
Her colour comes, and goes;
It trembles to a lily, —
It wavers to a rose.

The Ladies of St. James's

Henry Austin Dobson (1840-1921) was an accomplished writer of light verse, and some of his best work appeared in *Vignettes in Rhyme, Proverbs in Porcelain* and *Old World Idylls*.

John Dryden

All human things are subject to decay,
And, when fate summons, monarchs must obey.

Mac Flecknoe

None but the brave deserves the fair.

Alexander's Feast

Happy the man, and happy he alone,
He who can call today his own:
He who, secure within, can say,
To-morrow do thy worst, for I have lived to-day.

Translation of Horace

John Dryden (1631-1700) was born at Aldwinkle, Northants, and went to London in 1657. In 1659 he published *Heroic Stanzas* in memory of Oliver Cromwell, but he hastened to celebrate the Restoration with *Astraea Redux*. He produced many plays and much other work, but at the Revolution of 1688 was deprived of the laureateship to which he had been appointed in 1668 because he was a Roman Catholic. Dryden was the greatest literary figure of his age.

Marie Jeanne Becu Du Barry

After all, the world is but an amusing theatre, and I see no reason why a pretty woman should not play a principal part in it.

We learn to howl in the society of wolves.

Marie Jeanne Becu Du Barry (1743-93), daughter of a dressmaker, married the Comte Guillaume Du Barry and was presented at Court, where she soon became Mistress of Louis XV of France. She is said to have been strikingly handsome, not without wit, and frank to the point of vulgarity. She exercised great influence on Louis, but on his death she was banished to a convent. At the Revolution she fled to London, but returned to Paris in 1793, when she was arrested and guillotined.

Jonathan Edwards

The bodies of those that made such a noise and tumult when alive, when dead, lie as quietly among the graves of their neighbours as any others.

Procrastination

Jonathan Edwards (1703-58) was a New England philosopher and an ardent divine and formidable preacher. His principal philosophical work *A Careful and Strict Enquiry into the Modern Prevailing Notions of ... Freedom of Will* caused Johnson to say 'All theory is against freedom of the will; all experience for it.'

Elizabeth 1, Queen of England

If thy heart fails thee, climb not at all.

Lines written on a window after Sir Walter Raleigh's own 'Fain would I climb, yet fear to fall'

I know I have the body of a weak and feeble woman, but I have the heart and stomach of a king, and of a king of England too.

Speech to the Troops at Tilbury on the approach of the Armada, 1588

Elizabeth 1 (1533-1603), Queen of England and the daughter of Henry VIII and Anne Boleyn, was born at Greenwich. During Mary's reign Elizabeth's Protestant sympathies brought her under suspicion, and she lived at Hatfield until she became Queen in 1558. Her reign lasted forty-five years, and its glories are one of the main themes of English history.

Gracie Fields

People are always sending me pictures of their aspidistras.

10.9.1978

Gracie Fields (1898-1979) was an English comedienne.
Born Gracie Stansfield in Rochdale, she appeared in
London in *Mr. Tower of London*, which gave over 4,000
performances. Later she became a popular motion-picture
actress and singer.

James Elroy Flecker

I have seen old ships sail like swans asleep
Beyond the village which men still call Tyre.

The Old Ships

Away, for we are ready to a man!
Our camels sniff the evening and are glad.
Lead on, O Master of the Caravan:
Lead on the Merchant Princes of Bagdad.

The Golden Road to Samarkand

Have we not Indian carpets dark as wine,
Turbans and sashes, gowns and bows and veils,
And broideries of intricate design,
And printed hangings in enormous bales?

The Golden Road to Samarkand

Sweet to ride forth at evening from the wells,
When shadows pass gigantic on the sand,
And softly through the silence beat the bells
Along the Golden Road to Samarkand.

The Golden Road to Samarkand

James Elroy Flecker (1884-1915) entered the Consular
service and was posted first to Constantinople and then to
Beirut. He published *The Bridge of Fire, Forty-Two
Poems, The Golden Journey to Samarkand* and *The Old
Ships*. Two plays, *Hassan* and *Don Juan*, were published
posthumously.

Michael Foot

I had better recall, before someone else does, that I said on one occasion that all was fair in love, war, and parliamentary procedure.

7.9.1975

More Governments, including left-wing Governments, have been thrown out of power through a failure to deal with inflation than through any other single cause.

18.4.1978

What politics is all about is to try to combine protection of your principles with effective action. It is no use having effective action if you do not protect your principles.

On being voted Leader of
the Labour Party, 10.11.1980

The Right Hon Michael Foot (1913-), son of the late Sir Isaac Foot, has been MP for Ebbw Vale since 1960. He became Deputy Leader of the Labour Party in 1976 and was voted Leader of the Opposition upon the resignation of James Callaghan in 1980. He held the post of assistant editor of the *Tribune* in 1937/8, was acting editor of the *Evening Standard* in 1942, and political columnist of the *Daily Herald* from 1944 until 1964.

W. S. Gilbert

When I was a lad I served a term
As office-boy to an Attorney's firm.
I cleaned the windows and I swept the floor,
And I polished up the handle of the big front door.

HMS Pinafore

Sir William Schwenk Gilbert (1836-1911), the British humorist and dramatist, collaborated with Sir Arthur Sullivan in a great series of comic-operas, the popularity of them being due as much to Gilbert's lyrics as to Sullivan's music. Unfortunately, personal relationships between the two men became cool, and the partnership broke down owing to temperamental incompatability.

Johann Wolfgang Von Goethe

Know you the land where the lemon-trees bloom?
In the dark foliage the golden oranges glow; a soft wind
hovers from the sky, the myrtle is still and the laurel stands
tall.

Wilhelm Meisters Lehrjahre

Johann Wolfgang Von Goethe (1749-1832), the German
poet and man of letters, statesman and natural
philosopher, discovered his poetic vocation while studying
law at Leipzig. He met Herder at Strasbourg and became
leader of the Storm and Stress movement. Later he moved
to Weimar and entered the service of Duke Karl August.
The first part of his *Faust* appeared in 1808, but the second
part was not published until 1831.

Oliver Goldsmith

When lovely woman stoops to folly,
And finds too late that men betray,
What charm can soothe her melancholy,
What art can wash her guilt away?

The Vicar of Wakefield

Sweet Auburn! loveliest village of the plain.

The Deserted Village

A man he was to all the country dear,
And passing rich with forty pounds a year.

The Deserted Village

Here lies David Garrick, describe me, who can,
An abridgement of all that was pleasant in man.

Retaliation

On the stage he was natural, simple, affecting;
'Twas only that when he was off he was acting [Garrick].

Retaliation

I love everything that's old; old friends, old times, old
manners, old books, old wines.

She Stoops to Conquer

Oliver Goldsmith (1728-74) was born in Ireland, the son of a clergyman. He was educated at Trinity College, Dublin, then went to Edinburgh to study medicine. Later he went abroad and wandered through France, Switzerland and Italy, then returned to England and wrote his *History of England* and *Animated Nature*. Upon meeting Johnson he became a member of his 'Club', established his reputation with his poem *The Traveller*, and followed it with some collected essays, *The Vicar of Wakefield*, *The Deserted Village* and *She Stoops to Conquer*.

Thomas Gray

The curfew tolls the knell of parting day,
The lowing herd winds slowly o'er the lea,
The ploughman homeward plods his weary way,
And leaves the world to darkness and to me.

Elegy written in a Country Churchyard

Full many a flower is born to blush unseen,
And waste its sweetness on the desert air.

Elegy written in a Country Churchyard

Not all that tempts your wand'ring eyes
And heedless hearts, is lawful prize;
Nor all that glisters, gold.

Ode on the Death of a Favourite Cat

. . . Where ignorance is bliss
'Tis folly to be wise.

Ode on a Distant Prospect of Eton College

Thomas Gray (1716-71) was born in London. At Eton he formed a close friendship with Horace Walpole and together they went on a tour of France and Italy. Upon his return, Gray lived again in London, but visited his mother and sister at Stoke Poges. For some time he wrote poems which appeared anonymously in Dodsley's *Miscellany*, but in 1750 he wrote the now famous *Elegy written in a Country Churchyard*. The location was presumed to be Stoke Poges.

27

Joyce Grenfell

If I should go before the rest of you
Break not a flower nor inscribe a stone,
Nor when I'm gone speak in a Sunday voice
But be the usual selves that I have known.

Quoted in 'Radio Times' 1.1.1981

Weep if you must,
Parting is hell,
But life goes on,
So sing as well.

Quoted in 'Radio Times' 1.1.1981

Joyce Grenfell (1910-79), comedienne, film-star, expert at writing and speaking monologues, panellist on Joseph Cooper's 'Face the Music' programmes — Joyce Grenfell was all this and much more. Her books very quickly became bestsellers, and gave the fascinating story of her life.

Thomas Hardy

This is the weather the cuckoo likes,
And so do I:
When showers betumble the chestnut spikes
And nestlings fly;
And the little brown nightingale bills his best,
And they sit outside at the 'Traveller's Rest'.

Weathers

And maids come forth sprig-muslin drest,
And citizens dream of the south and west,
And so do I.

Weathers

Sweet cyder is a great thing,
A great thing to me,
Spinning down to Weymouth town
By Ridgway thirstily,
And maid and mistress summoning,
Who tend the hostely —

Great Things

Thomas Hardy (1840-1928) became widely known and acclaimed as the Wessex author. Born at Bockhampton near Dorchester, he wrote *Far From the Madding Crowd* and *Under the Greenwood Tree* there before moving away and writing *The Return of the Native, The Mayor of Casterbridge* and others, including his famous *Tess of the D'Urbervilles*. He also wrote many poems.

Joel Chandler Harris

Oh, whar shill we go w'en de great day comes,
Wid de blowin' er de trumpits en de bangin' er de drums?
How many po' sinners'll be kotched out late
En find no latch ter de golden gate?

Uncle Remus, His Songs

Joel Chandler Harris (1848-1908), the American writer, was born in Georgia and first published his *Uncle Remus* stories in the Atlanta *Constitution* which he edited from 1890 to 1905. The tales were written in Negro dialect and gained worldwide popularity. His autobiography *On the Plantation* was published in 1892.

William Hazlitt

Give me the clear blue sky over my head, and the green turf beneath my feet, a winding road before me, and a three hours' march to dinner.

Table Talk: On Going a Journey

William Hazlitt (1778-1830) dabbled in portrait painting, but took to writing on the advice of Coleridge. He then went to London where he contributed to the press and various magazines. He became famous for, amongst other works, *Table Talk* and *The Spirit of the Age*.

Felicia Dorothea Hemans

The boy stood on the burning deck
Whence all but he had fled;
The flame that lit the battle's wreck
Shone round him o'er the dead.

Casabianca

There came a burst of thunder sound –
The boy – oh, where was he?

Casabianca

The stately homes of England,
How beautiful they stand!
Amidst their tall ancestral trees,
O'er all the pleasant land.

The Homes of England

Felicia Dorothea Hemans (1793-1835), a British poet, was born in Liverpool. She published many volumes of sentimental verse which attained great popularity, but her best known poem is *Casabianca*.

William Ernest Henley

It matters not how strait the gate,
How charged with punishments the scroll,
I am the master of my fate:
I am the captain of my soul.

*Echoes: Invictus. In Memoriam of
R. T. Hamilton Bruce*

Under the bludgeonings of chance
My head is bloody, but unbowed.

*Echoes: Invictus. In
Memoriam of R. T. Hamilton Bruce*

A late lark twitters from the quiet skies.

*Echoes: In Memoriam of
Margaritae Sororis*

What have I done for you,
England, my England?
What is there I would not do,
England, my own?

For England's Sake, iii. Pro Rege Nostro

William Ernest Henley (1849-1903) was born at Gloucester. Tuberculosis and the subsequent amputation of a left leg left him crippled from boyhood. He wrote much verse, criticism, and miscellaneous journalism, and was closely associated with Stevenson, with whom he wrote *Deacon Brodie* and other plays.

Robert Herrick

I sing of brooks, of blossoms, birds and bowers;
Of April, May, of June and July flowers . . .
Hesperides: The Argument of His Book

Gather ye rosebuds while ye may
Old Time is still a-flying . . .
Hesperides: To the Virgins

Robert Herrick (1591-1674) was born in Cheapside,
London, and was a friend of Ben Jonson. In 1629 he
became vicar of Dean Prior, near Totnes, and in 1648
published *Hesperides*, which was a collection of sacred and
pastoral poetry of unrivalled lyric quality.

Horace

He who has begun his task has half done it.
Epistles

If you do not know how to live aright, make way for those
who do . . . It is time for you to leave the scene.
Epistles

What shall be to-morrow, think not of asking. Each day
that Fortune gives you, be it what it may, set down for
gain.
Odes

The snows have scattered and fled; already the grass comes
again in the fields and the leaves on the trees.
Odes

Quintus Horatius Flaccus Horace (65-8BC), the Roman
poet, was born at Venusia in Apulia and was present on the
losing side at the battle of Philippi, but obtained his pardon
and returned to Rome. He was given a Sabine farm and
then wrote poems which included *Satires, Odes, Epistles*
and the *Ars Poetica*.

Joseph Joubert

What is left of human wisdom after age has purified it may
be the best we have.

One should choose for a wife only a woman one would choose for a friend if she were a man.

A clever talk between two men is a unison: between a man and a woman it is harmony: we come away satisfied by one, enchanted by the other.

He who has no poetry in himself will find poetry in nothing.

We must respect the past and mistrust the present if we are to safeguard the future.

It is better to turn over a question without deciding it than to decide it without turning it over.

The evening of life comes bearing its own lamp.

Joseph Joubert (1754-1824) was a French thinker and is famous for his posthumous work *Pensees, Essais Maximes* and *Correspondance*.

John Keats

Season of mists and mellow fruitfulness,
Close bosom-friend of the maturing sun.

To Autumn

To bend with apples the moss'd cottage-trees,
And fill all fruit with ripeness to the core.

To Autumn

A thing of beauty is a joy forever:
Its loveliness increases.

Endymion

I cannot see what flowers are at my feet,
Nor what soft incense hangs upon the boughs.

Ode to a Nightingale

'Beauty is truth, truth beauty,' – that is all
Ye know on earth, and all ye need to know.

Ode on a Grecian Urn

And there shall be for thee all soft delight.

Ode to Psyche

John Keats (1795-1821) was the son of a livery-stable keeper in London. He acquired a knowledge of Latin and history, and some French, was apprenticed to a surgeon and became a student at Guy's Hospital. However he soon abandoned medicine for poetry and was at first not very successful. Later he wrote *Endymion, The Eve of St. Agnes, La Belle Dame sans Merci* and the unfinished *Eve of St. Mark*. About the same time he wrote his great Odes *On a Grecian Urn, To a Nightingale* and *To Autumn*, as well as odes *On Melancholy, On Indolence* and *To Psyche*.

La Bruyère

Modesty is to merit what shadow is to the figures in a picture; it gives accent and strength.

Every vice falsely resembles some virtue, and it always takes advantage of the resemblance.

There is no trade in the world so toilsome as that of pursuing fame; life is over before the main part of your work has begun.

There are but three events which concern mankind; birth, life, and death. All know nothing of their birth, all submit to die, and many forget to live.

Jean de La Bruyère (1645-96), a French essayist, was born in Paris, studied law, took a post in the Revenue office, and in 1684 entered the service of the house of Condé. His *Caractères* (satirical portraits of contemporaries) made him many enemies.

La Rochefoucauld

If we cannot find peace within ourselves, it is useless to look for it elsewhere.

Passion often turns the cleverest man into an idiot and the greatest blockhead into someone clever.

It takes greater character to handle good fortune than bad.

Self-interest blinds some people and sharpens the eyesight of others.

To establish yourself in the world, do all you can to seem established already.

Francois, Duc de la Rochefoucauld (1613-80) was born in Paris, became a soldier and took part in the wars of the Fronde. His later years were divided between the Court and literary society. He is best known for his work *Réflexions, Sentences et Maximes Morales* (1665).

Emma Lazarus

Give me your tired, your poor,
Your huddled masses yearning to be free,
The wretched refuse of your teeming shore,
Send these, the homeless, tempest-tossed, to me;
I lift my lamp beside the golden door.
Lines inscribed on the Statue of Liberty

Emma Lazarus (1849-87), an American poet, essayist and philanthropist, was born in New York City. She published a number of works, including *Alide; An Episode of Goethe's Life* in 1874. She championed oppressed Jews during persecution in Russia, and wrote *Songs of a Semite*.

Edward Lear

'How pleasant to know Mr. Lear!'
Who has written such volumes of stuff!
Some think him ill-tempered and queer,
But a few think him pleasant enough.
Nonsense Songs: Preface

On the coast of Coromandel
Where the early pumpkins blow,
In the middle of the woods
Lived the Yonghy-Bonghy-Bò.
Two old chairs, and half a candle, —
One old jug without a handle, —
These were all his worldly goods.
*Nonsense Songs: The Courtship of
the Yonghy-Bonghy-Bò*

Edward Lear (1812-88), the British artist and humorist, first attracted attention with his paintings of birds, but later turned to painting landscapes. He travelled in Italy, Greece, Egypt and India and published books on his travels with his own illustrations. He published his *Book of Nonsense* in 1846, which he illustrated himself, and popularized the limerick.

Henry Wadsworth Longfellow

Then the little Hiawatha
Learned of every bird its language,
Learned their names and all their secrets,
How they built their nests in Summer,
Where they hid themselves in Winter,
Talked with them whene'er he met them,
Called them 'Hiawatha's chickens'.

Hiawatha's Childhood

Silently one by one, in the infinite meadows of heaven,
Blossomed the lovely stars, the forget-me-nots of the angels.

Evangeline

The heights by great men reached and kept
Were not attained by sudden flight,
But they, while their companions slept,
Were toiling upward in the night.

The Ladder of Saint Augustine

And the night shall be filled with music,
And the cares that infest the day,
Shall fold their tents like the Arabs,
And as silently steal away.

The Day is Done

Build me straight, O worthy Master!
Staunch and strong, a goodly vessel.

Thou, too, sail on, O Ship of State!

The Building of the Ship

Henry Wadsworth Longfellow (1807-82), the American poet, published his first volume of poems *Voices in the Night* in 1839 and *Ballads and Other Poems* in 1841.

These were soon followed by *Poems on Slavery, Hiawatha* (1855), *The Courtship of Miles Standish* and *Tales of a Wayside Inn*.

Anita Loos

Kissing your hand may make you feel very very good, but a diamond and sapphire bracelet lasts for ever.

Gentlemen Prefer Blondes

Anita Loos (1893-), the American humorous writer, collaborated with her husband in writing motion-picture scenarios, and was author of *Gentlemen Prefer Blondes* (1925) and *But Gentlemen Marry Brunettes (1928)*.

Samuel Lover

When once the itch of literature comes over a man, nothing can cure it but the scratching of a pen.

Handy Andy

Samuel Lover (1797-1868) was born in Dublin and became a painter of miniatures, but in 1835 he settled in London and conquered society by singing his own compositions. These he published as *Songs and Ballads*, but he is also remembered for his humorous novels *Rory O'More* and *Handy Andy*.

Edward George Bulwer-Lytton

Beneath the rule of men entirely great
The pen is mightier than the sword.

Richelieu

Revolutions are not made with rose-water.

The Parisians

Edward George Earle Lytton Bulwer-Lytton (1803-73), first Baron Lytton, was born in London. His father was a soldier and his mother a member of the old family of Lytton. He published his first poems in 1820, and later his novels followed every turn of the public taste. He became famous for *Falkland, Eugene Aram* and *The Last Days of Pompeii*, and as a playwright achieved success with *Richelieu*.

Groucho Marx

Saddest movie I've ever seen – I cried all the way through. Its sad when you're 82.

On 'Last Tango in Paris'

Groucho (Julius) Marx (1895-1977) was one of the four Marx Brothers, a team of American film comedians who started the Zeppo-Marx Agency in 1935 and appeared only in earlier films. They were known as Groucho (Julius), Harpo (Arthur), Chico (Leonard) and Zeppo (Herbert).

John Masefield

I must go down to the seas again, to the lonely sea and the sky,
And all I ask is a tall ship and a star to steer her by –

Sea Fever

And the wheel's kick and the wind's song and the white sail's shaking,
And a grey mist on the sea's face, and a grey dawn breaking.

Sea Fever

And all I ask is a merry yarn from a laughing fellow-rover,
And quiet sleep and a sweet dream when the long trek's over.

Sea Fever

John Masefield (1878-1967) was born in Ledbury, Herefordshire, ran away to sea, and while in the USA worked as a barman in New York. He returned to England and worked on the *Manchester Guardian*, then settled in London and attracted notice for some volumes of poetry. Fame came with his verse narrative *The Everlasting Mercy*, and he was later appointed poet laureate. He was awarded the OM in 1935.

John Milton

The mind is its own place, and in itself
Can make a heav'n of hell a hell of heav'n.

Paradise Lost

Fame is the spur that the clear spirit doth raise
(That last infirmity of noble mind)
To scorn delights and live laborious days.

Lycidas

Haste thee, Nymph, and bring with thee
Jest and youthful jollity,
Quips and cranks, and wanton wiles,
Nods, and becks, and wreathed smiles.

L'Allegro

Sport that wrinkled Care derides,
And Laughter holding both his sides.
Come and trip it as ye go
On the light fantastic toe.

L'Allegro

John Milton (1604-74), son of a scrivener and composer of music, was educated at St Paul's School and Christ's College, Cambridge. He became a BA in 1629 and an MA in 1632. After leaving Cambridge he lived with his father at Horton in Buckinghamshire, and whilst there he read the classics and prepared himself for his vocation as a poet. After the execution of Charles 1, he published *Tenure of Kings and Magistrates*, and was then appointed Latin secretary to the newly-formed Council of State. He became blind but retained his post as Latin secretary until the Restoration, when he was arrested and fined. He was soon released, but lost the greater part of his fortune.

Montaigne

The greatest thing in the world is to know how to be sufficient unto oneself.

The strength of any plan depends on timing.

We are all made up of fragments, so shapelessly and strangely assembled that every moment, every piece plays its own game. There is as much difference between us and ourselves as between us and others.

A learned man is not learned in all things; but an able man is able in all, even in ignorance.

No man is exempt from saying silly things. The misfortune is to say them seriously.

Dying is the greatest task we have to do, but practice can give us no assistance.

Michel Eyquem de Montaigne (1533-92), the French essayist, was born at the Chateau de Montaigne near Bordeaux. He studied law and became a councillor of the Bordeaux parlement. For a time he frequented the Court of Francis 11, but eventually retired to his estates and wrote several volumes of *Essays*.

William Morris

Forget six counties overhung with smoke,
Forget the snorting steam and piston stroke,
Forget the spreading of the hideous town;
Think rather of the pack-horse on the down,
And dream of London small and white and clean,
The clear Thames bordered by its gardens green.
Prologue to Earthly Paradise

William Morris (1834-96), the British poet and craftsman, was born at Walthamstow and was educated at Marlborough School and Exeter College, Oxford, where he formed a lasting friendship with Edward Burne-Jones the painter and designer and was influenced by Ruskin and Rossetti. *The Earthly Paradise* was written in 1868-70, but a visit to Iceland in 1871 inspired his greatest poem *Sigurd the Volsung* and his translations of the Sagas.

Ogden Nash

The ant has made himself illustrious
Through constant industry industrious.

The trouble with a kitten is that
Eventually it becomes a CAT.

Tell me, O Octopus, I begs,
Is those things arms, or is they legs?

Candy
Is dandy,
But liquor
Is quicker.

Reflections on Ice-breaking

Ogden Nash (1902-71) was an American poet, born in Rye, NY. He published numerous volumes of humorous verse which had impeccable technique and quietly-puncturing satire.

Sir Henry John Newbolt

Take my drum to England, hang et by the shore,
Strike et when your powder's runnin' low —
The Island Race: Drake's Drum

There's a breathless hush in the Close to-night —
Ten to make and the match to win —
A bumping pitch and a blinding light,
An hour to play and the last man in.
The Island Race: Vitaï Lampada

Sir Henry John Newbolt (1862-1938) was a British poet and also a barrister, but he was an authority on naval matters and wrote *The Year of Trafalgar* (1905) and *A Naval History of the War, 1914-18* (1920). His *Songs of the Sea* and *Songs of the Fleet* were set to music by Sir Charles Villiers Stanford, the Irish composer.

Sir Isaac Newton

I do not know what I may appear to the world, but to myself I seem to have been only like a boy playing on the sea-shore.

Brewsters' Memoirs of Newton

Sir Isaac Newton (1642-1727), the British philosopher, was educated at Grantham Grammar School and Trinity College, Cambridge. He discovered the binomial theorem and the differential and integral calculus and began to investigate the phenomena of universal gravitation. Soon he published his *New Theory about Light and Colours.* Later he published (with Halley) his greatest work *Philosophiae Naturalis Principia Mathematica* (1687).

Alfred Noyes

The wind was a torrent of darkness among the gusty trees,
The moon was a ghostly galleon tossed upon cloudy seas,
The road was a ribbon of moonlight over the purple moor,
And the highwayman came riding –
The highwayman came riding, up to the old inn door.

The Highwayman

Come down to Kew in lilac-time, it isn't far from London –
And you shall wander hand in hand with love in summer's
wonderland.

The Barrel-Organ

Alfred Noyes (1880-1958) was a British poet who was
educated at Oxford and later became professor of modern
English literature at Princeton University. His best-known
poems include *The Highwayman* and *The Barrel Organ*,
but he also wrote *Drake*, *The Torch Bearers* and *The
Accusing Ghost*, which was an attempt to clear the name of
Roger Casement.

John Owen

God and the doctor we alike adore
But only when in danger, not before;
The danger o'er, both are alike requited,
God is forgotten, and the doctor slighted.

Epigrams

Times change, and we change with them too.

Epigrams

John Owen (1560?-1622), the Welsh epigrammatist, was a
master of Latin idioms and the author of a number of
shrewd and pointed epigrams.

Robert Owen

All the world is queer save thee and me, and even thou art a
little queer.

*On separating from his business
partner, William Allen, in 1828*

41

Robert Owen (1771-1858) became a British socialist and co-operator, and manager of a mill at New Lanark where, by improving working and housing conditions and by providing schools, he created a model community. Later he organised the Grand National Consolidated Trades Union, and his ideas did much to stimulate the co-operative movement.

Dorothy Parker

Congratulations: we all knew you had it in you.

> *Telegram to a friend who had*
> *just had a baby*

She ran the whole gamut of her emotions, from A to B.

> *Remark about an actress*

Byron and Shelley and Keats
Were a trio of lyrical treats.
The forehead of Shelley was cluttered with curls,
And Keats never was a descendant of earls,
And Byron walked out with a number of girls . . .

> *The Lives and Times of Keats,*
> *Shelley and Byron*

Four be the things I'd be better without,
Love, curiosity, freckles, and doubt.

> *Inventory*

O, is it then, Utopian
To hope that I may meet a man
Who'll not relate, in accents suave,
The tales of girls he used to have?

> *De Profundis*

Dorothy Parker (1893-1967), the American writer, was born in the West End of New Jersey and was a member of the Rothschild family. She married and became Mrs Alan Campbell. She wrote much verse, some of it collected in *Enough Rope* (1926), *Sunset Gun* (1928), *Death and Taxes* (1931), and a number of short stories, including *Laments for the Living, After Such Pleasures* and *Here Lies*.

Blaise Pascal

The heart has its reasons which reason knows nothing of.

Imagination is the deceitful part of man, a mistress of error and falsity who cheats us the more because she does not cheat us always.

If you want people to think well of you, do not speak well of yourself.

Can anything be more ridiculous than that a man should have the right to kill me because he lives on the other side of the water and because his ruler has a quarrel with mine?

Blaise Pascal (1623-62), the French philosopher and mathematician, was a precocious student. He investigated the laws governing the weight of air, the equilibrium of liquids, the hydraulic press, the infinitesimal calculus, and the mathematical theory of probability.

James Payn

I had never had a piece of toast
Particularly long and wide,
But fell upon the sanded floor
And always on the buttered side.

Chambers's Journal

James Payn (1830-98), the English novelist, was editor of *Chambers's Journal* from 1859 to 1874, and of *The Cornhill Magazine* from 1883 to 1896. He was also author of a number of novels including *Lost Sir Massingberd*.

Samuel Pepys

I went out to Charing Cross, to see Major-general Harrison hanged, drawn and quartered; which was done there, he looking as cheerful as any man could do in that condition.

Diary, 13.10.1660

Samuel Pepys (1633-1703) was appointed secretary to the Admiralty in 1672. Stationed in London, he was therefore in a position to know everything of importance taking place in England. He kept his personal *Diary* until failing eyesight forced him to stop. Because it was in Pepys' own version of Shelton's shorthand the *Diary* was consequently not deciphered and published until 1825.

William Pitt

Confidence is a plant of slow growth in an aged bosom; youth the season of credulity.

Speech in House of Commons, 14.1.1766

The poorest man may in his cottage bid defiance to all the forces of the crown. It may be frail – its roof may shake – the wind may blow through it – the storm may enter – but the King of England may not enter . . .

Speech on the Excise Bill

William Pitt (1708-78), first Earl of Chatham, entered Parliament as MP for Old Sarum and gained a reputation for himself by his attacks on the Prime Minister, Sir Robert Walpole. For a time he was Paymaster-General. He helped to form the ministry which continued the war against the French (Seven Years' War), and was largely responsible for the British victories in Canada, India, and on the seas.

Alexander Pope

Happy the man whose wish and care
A few paternal acres bound,
Content to breathe his native air,
In his own ground.

Ode on Solitude

Words are like leaves; and where they most abound,
Much fruit of sense beneath is rarely found.

An Essay on Criticism

Be not the first by whom the new are tried,
Nor yet the last to lay the old aside.

An Essay on Criticism

To err is human, to forgive, divine.

An Essay on Criticism

Hope springs eternal in the human breast;
Man never is, but always to be blest.

An Essay on Man

For fools rush in where angels fear to tread.

An Essay on Criticism

Alexander Pope (1688-1744) was the son of a Roman Catholic linen-draper of London. A severe illness at the age of twelve ruined his health and distorted his figure, but he showed his literary skill in his *Pastorals* when he was sixteen. He became known to Joseph Addison's circle and soon published his *Messiah*, which was followed by his *Rape of the Lock*. His *Ode for Music on St. Cecilia's Day* was not very successful, but he also published *Windsor Forest* which was well received. He moved from Addison's circle and became a member of the Scriblerus Club, an association which included Swift, Gay, Arbuthnot and other famous writers.

Richard Porson

I went to Frankfort where I got drunk
With that most learn'd professor, Brunck;
I went to Worms, and got more drunken
With that more learn'd professor, Ruhnken.

Facetiae Cantabrigienses, 1825

Richard Porson (1759-1808), a Regius professor of Greek at Cambridge, edited four plays of *Euripides*. His finest single piece of criticism was his supplement to the preface to his *Hecuba*. His elucidation of Greek idiom and usage and his editing of texts advanced Greek scholarship.

Ronald Reagan

I don't think anyone would cheerfully want to use atomic weapons – but the enemy should go to bed every night being afraid that we might.

*Remark in July 1967, during
a grim period of the Vietnam War*

All of us were expecting it to be a cliffhanger.

*Surprised remark on being elected
Republican President of US, November 1980*

Ronald Reagan (1911-) began his career as an actor in America in the thirties, starred in fifty films, and later became well known on television. In 1967 he became Republican Governor of California. In 1968 he made a bid for the Republican presidential nomination, which was unsuccessful, but in 1980, by a landslide victory, he was elected 40th President of the USA, to succeed President Carter in that office on 20 January 1981.

George Robey

I am satiated with fishing stories – there's no truth in them! The man who caught that fish is a blasted liar.

Comment on seeing a stuffed fish in a glass case

(Sir) George Robey (1869-1954) was the stage-name of British comedian George Edward Wade. Posing as 'The Prime Minister of Mirth' and dressed in close-buttoned frock-coat and semi-clerical bowler, he sang such songs as 'Tempt Me Not'. He was a master of significant gesture and voice inflection, and was distinguished by his bushy eyebrows.

Mickey Rooney

I'm learning every day. Life wouldn't be any fun if it didn't have its ups and downs.

In an interview for 'Woman's Realm'

It isn't how tall you are. It's what you do with yourself that counts.

In an interview for 'Woman's Realm'

Mickey Rooney (1920-) was a working actor from the age of fifteen months, and first appeared in Vaudeville with his parents. He later became a businessman and worked for dozens of companies. A much-married man, Mickey Rooney had had eight wives up until 1980, beating even Henry VIII's record!

Christina Rossetti

Better by far you should forget and smile
Than that you should remember and be sad.

Remember

My heart is like a singing bird
Whose nest is in a watered shoot;
My heart is like an apple-tree
Whose boughs are bent with thickset fruit;
My heart is like a rainbow shell
That paddles in a halcyon sea;
My heart is gladder than all these
Because my love is come to me.

A Birthday

Christina Georgina Rossetti (1830-94), the British poet
and sister of Dante Gabriel Rossetti the poet and artist,
was a devout Anglican. She produced much popular lyric
and religious verse.

George Sand

We cannot tear out a single page from our life, but we can
throw the whole book into the fire.

Life is a slate where all our sins are written; from time to
time we rub the sponge of repentance over it so we can
begin sinning again.

George Sand (1804-76) was the pseudonym of French
novelist Armandine Aurore Lucile Dupin, who married
young but separated from her husband and lived in Paris
as a writer. Subsequent relations with Alfred de Musset
and Chopin were to influence her work.

Robert Falcon Scott

We are in a desperate state, feet frozen etc. No fuel and a
long way from food, but it would do your heart good to be
in our tent, to hear our songs and the cheery conversation.
Farewell letter to Sir J. M. Barrie

For God's sake look after our people.
Journal, 25.3.1912

Had we lived, I should have had a tale to tell of the
hardihood, endurance and courage of my companions
which would have stirred the heart of every Englishman.

These rough notes and our dead bodies must tell the tale.

Robert Falcon Scott (1868-1912), the British Antarctic explorer, entered the navy in 1882. Later he commanded two Antarctic expeditions, first in the *Discovery* (1901-4) and then in the *Terra Nova* (1910-12). On 18 January 1912 he reached the South Pole, only to discover that the Norwegian explorer Amundsen had already been there. On the return journey he and his companions, Wilson, Oates, Bowers, and Evans, perished. His journal was recovered and published. His son Peter is well known as a naturalist and for his paintings of birds.

William Shakespeare

All the world's a stage
And all the men and women merely players:
They have their exits and their entrances;
And one man in his time plays many parts.

As You Like It

Neither a borrower, nor a lender be;
For loan oft loses both itself and friend,
And borrowing dulls the edge of husbandry.

Hamlet

This above all: to thine own self be true,
And it must follow, as the night the day,
Thou canst not then be false to any man.

Hamlet

Let me have men about me that are fat;
Sleek-headed men and such as sleep o' nights:
Yond Cassius has a lean and hungry look;
He thinks too much — such men are dangerous.

Julius Caesar

Smooth runs the water where the brook is deep.

King Henry VI

How far that little candle throws his beams!
So shines a good deed in a naughty world.

The Merchant of Venice

I'll put a girdle round the earth,
In forty minutes.

A Midsummer Night's Dream

Lord, what fools these mortals be!
A Midsummer Night's Dream

Night's candles are burnt out, and jocund day
Stands on tiptoe on the misty mountain tops.
Romeo and Juliet

If music be the food of love, play on.
Twelfth Night

Be not afraid of greatness; some are born great, some achieve greatness, and some have greatness thrust upon them.
Twelfth Night

William Shakespeare (1564-1616) was born at Stratford-upon-Avon and educated at the free Grammar School. He left Stratford in about 1582 and went to London where he joined a company of players and soon became established as an actor and playwright. His plays brought him immediate fame. His output was prolific and his collected works as published today contain 37 plays, 2 long poems, and 154 sonnets. The plays are divided into 17 comedies, 10 histories, and 10 tragedies. He basked in the favour of Queen Elizabeth I and her successor, King James I, but eventually ceased to write and retired once again to Stratford-upon-Avon.

George Bernard Shaw

You think that you are Ann's suitor: that you are the pursuer and she the pursued. Fool: it is you who are the pursued, the marked-down quarry, the destined prey.
Man and Superman

A man is like a phonograph with half a dozen records. You soon get tired of them all.
Getting Married

Marriage is popular because it combines the maximum of temptation with the maximum of opportunity.
Maxims for Revolutionists

Home is the girl's prison and the woman's workhouse.
Man and Superman

Go anywhere in England, where there are natural, wholesome, contented, and really nice English people; and what do you always find? That the stables are the real centre of the household.

Heartbreak House

Nothing is ever done in this world until men are prepared to kill one another if it is not done.

Major Barbara

George Bernard Shaw (1856-1950), the son of a civil servant, left Ireland and came to London, where he became a brilliant debater among the Fabians. He wrote five novels, then became a playwright and consequently met with great success. His comedy *Pygmalion* was written especially for Mrs Patrick Campbell, and his letters to the actress Ellen Terry are of great interest.

Samuel Smiles

The shortest way to do many things is to do only one thing at once.

We often discover what *will* do, by finding out what will not do; and probably he who never made a mistake never made a discovery.

Self-Help

A place for everything, and everything in its place.

Thrift

Samuel Smiles (1812-1904) was born at Haddington and educated at Haddington Grammar School and Edinburgh University. He became in turn a doctor, journalist, and secretary to railway companies, but he achieved fame with his *Life of George Stephenson* and the popular didactic work *Self-Help*, published in 1859.

Logan Pearsall Smith

Thank heaven, the sun has gone in, and I don't have to go out and enjoy it.

All Trivia: Last words

There are two things to aim at in life: first, to get what you want; and, after that, to enjoy it. Only the wisest of mankind achieve the second.

Afterthoughts: Life and Human Nature

Logan Pearsall Smith (1865-1946), born in Philadelphia, was an essayist who spent most of his life in England. He was the author of *The Youth of Parnassus* (1895) and many other works, including *Songs and Sonnets* and *Milton and his Modern Critics* (1940).

Edmund Spenser

Sweet Thames, run softly, till I end my song.

Prothalamion

At length they all to merry London came,
To merry London, my most kindly nurse,
That to me gave this life's first native source.

Prothalamion

Sleep after toil, port after stormy seas,
Ease after war, death after life does greatly please.

The Faerie Queene: Book 1

And all for love, and nothing for reward.

The Faerie Queene: Book 2

Edmund Spenser (1552-92) was born in London, educated at Cambridge, and then entered the service of the Earl of Leicester. In 1580 he became secretary to the Lord Deputy in Ireland and while at Kilcolman Castle completed the first three books of *The Faerie Queene*. Kilcolman Castle was burnt down by rebels and Spenser and his family narrowly escaped. The last six books of *The Faerie Queene* were lost, probably destroyed in the fire at the Castle.

Madame de Staël

Politeness is the art of selecting among one's real thoughts.

Liberty is the only thing that at all times and in every country is in one's blood. Liberty and — what cannot be separated from it — love of one's country.

Life may often seem like a long shipwreck of which the debris are friendship, glory, and love. The shores of our existence are strewn with them.

Anne Louise Germaine de Staël (1766-1817), a French author, was born in Paris, the daughter of the financier Jacques Necker, and married the Baron de Staël-Holstein in 1785. An ardent advocate of political freedom, she was banished from Paris by Napoleon, but settled at Coppet on Lake Geneva and gathered around her men like A. W. von Schlegel, Byron, and Benjamin Constant. Her most influential work was *De l'Allemagne,* which revealed to France the richness of German literature.

Philip Dormer Stanhope

Be wiser than other people if you can, but do not tell them so.
Letters to his Son, 19.11.1745

An injury is much sooner forgotten than an insult.
Letters to his Son, 9.10.1746

I recommend you to take care of the minutes: for hours will take care of themselves.
Letters to his Son, 6.11.1747

Idleness is only the refuge of weak minds.
Letters to his Son, 20.7.1749

Philip Dormer Stanhope (1694-1773), fourth Earl of Chesterfield, was an opponent of Walpole and upon the latter's death became Lord Lieutenant of Ireland in 1745 and a Secretary of State in 1746. He was associated with Swift, Pope, and Bolingbroke, and is remembered chiefly for his *Letters to his Son.*

Stendhal

The better you know mankind, the more you are able to overlook the little shortcomings of your friends.

Nothing is less certain than success.

The world is full of people who can't bear being alone and to whom any remark, however uninteresting it may be, is better than nothing at all.

Heroes have intervals of fear, cowards moments of bravery, and virtuous women moments of weakness.

Stendhal (1783-1842) was the pseudonym of the French novelist Marie Henri Beyle. Born in Grenoble, he served in the ill-fated Russian campaign. Failing in his hopes of being a prefect, he lived in Italy from 1814, but suspicion of espionage drove him back to Paris, where he supported himself by literary hack-work. Balzac favourably reviewed his *La Chartreuse de Parme,* and from 1830 he was a member of the consular service.

R. L. Stevenson

Politics is perhaps the only profession for which no preparation is thought necessary.

Even if the doctor does not give you a year, even if he hesitates about a month, make one brave push and see what can be accomplished in a week.

Go, little book, and wish to all,
Flowers in the garden, meat in the hall,
A bin of wine, a spice of wit,
A house with lawns enclosing it,
A living river by the door,
A nightingale in the sycamore!

Underwoods: 1. Envoy

Robert Louis Stevenson (1850-94) published his *Inland Voyage* in 1878 and *Travels with a Donkey in the Cevennes* the following year. Despite ill health, he then contributed to a number of periodicals. He also wrote a number of essays, short stories, and fragments of travel and autobiography. After writing *Treasure Island, The Strange Case of Dr. Jekyll and Mr. Hyde, Kidnapped, Catriona, The Black Arrow* and *The Master of Ballantrae,* he wrote some remarkable poetry, which was collected in *A Child's Garden of Verses* and *Underwoods.*

Tagore

God, the great giver, can open the whole universe to our gaze in the narrow space of a single lane.

Sir Rabindranath Tagore (1861-1941) was an Indian poet and a Nobel Prize-winner in 1913. His works are marked by deep religious feeling and a strong sense of the beauty of earth and sky in his native land, as well as his love of childhood. This is shown particularly in his poem *The Crescent Moon*. Tagore wrote mainly in Bengali, but he also wrote in English and translated into English some of his own Indian works.

Sir Thomas Talfourd

'Tis a little thing
To give a cup of water; yet its draught
Of cool refreshment, drain'd by fever'd lips,
May give a shock of pleasure to the frame
More exquisite than when nectarean juice
Renews the life of joy in happiest hours.

Ion

Sir Thomas Noon Talfourd (1795-1854) was a judge and author but made little impression himself. He is principally remembered as the friend of Charles Lamb, whose *Letters* and *Memorials* he published in 1837 and 1848, although Charles Lamb died in 1834.

Charles Maurice de Talleyrand

They have learnt nothing, and forgotten nothing.
*Attributed to Talleyrand by the
Chevalier du Pan, Jan 1796*

It is the beginning of the end.
*Remark to Napoleon after the
battle of Leipzig, 18.10.1813*

War is much too serious a thing to be left to military men.

You do not play whist, sir? Alas, what a sad old age you are preparing for yourself.

When reproached for his addiction to cards

Black as the devil,
Hot as hell,
Pure as an angel,
Sweet as love.

Talleyrand's recipe for coffee

Charles Maurice de Talleyrand (1754-1838) was a French statesman. He was born in Paris and was a supporter of modern reform, but fled to the USA during the Terror of the French Revolution. He returned to France in 1796 and served as Foreign Minister under the Directory from 1778-9, continuing under Napoleon from 1799 to 1807. He represented France at the Congress of Vienna (1814-15), and was ambassador to London from 1830 to 1834.

Alfred, Lord Tennyson

I climb the hill: from end to end
Of all the landscape underneath,
I find no place that does not breathe
Some gracious memory of my friend.

In Memoriam (of Arthur Hallam)

'Tis better to have loved and lost
Then never to have loved at all.

In Memoriam (of Arthur Hallam)

Kind hearts are more than coronets,
And simple faith than Norman blood.

Lady Clara Vere de Vere

Knowledge comes, but wisdom lingers.

Locksley Hall

In the Spring a young man's fancy lightly turns to thoughts of love.

Locksley Hall

A lie which is half a truth is ever the blackest of lies,
A lie which is all a lie may be met and fought with outright,
But a lie which is part a truth is a harder matter to fight.

The Grandmother

The gods themselves cannot recall their gifts.

Tithonus

Alfred, first Baron Tennyson (1809-92), was educated at
Trinity College Cambridge, where he became acquainted
with A. H. Hallam. He won the chancellor's medal for
English verse in 1829 with a poem called *Timbuctoo*. In
1832 he travelled with Hallam on the Continent, but
Hallam died in 1833 and Tennyson immediately began his
poem *In Memoriam* expressing grief for his dead friend.
This was followed by many poems and *The Idylls of the
King*.

Dylan Thomas

In the sun that is young once only,
Time let me play and be
Golden in the mercy of his means.

Fern Hill

And green and golden I was huntsman and herdsman.

Fern Hill

In the sun born over and over,
I ran my heedless ways,
My wishes raced through the house high hay,
And nothing I cared . . .

Fern Hill

The force that drives the water through the rocks
Drives my red blood.

*The Force that through the
Green fuse drives the Flower*

Nothing grows in our garden, only washing. And babies.

Under Milk Wood

Dylan Thomas (1914-53) was born in Swansea, the son of
the English master at the local school where he was
educated. Beginning as a reporter on the *South Wales*

Evening Post, he later became a journalist in London, and published his volume *Eighteen Poems* in 1934. He reached mastery of his medium in *Deaths and Entrances* and *Under Milk Wood,* and his short stories entitled *Portrait of the Artist as a Young Dog* are autobiographical. He died in New York while on a series of reading and lecture tours.

James Thomson

Give a man a pipe he can smoke,
Give a man a book he can read;
And his home is bright with a calm delight,
Though the room be poor indeed.

Gifts

James Thomson (1834-82), the child of poor parents, made friends with Charles Bradlaugh, the English free-thinker and politician, wrote for the *National Reformer,* and took an active part in the propaganda of free thought. His chief poem was *The City of Dreadful Night.* It was contributed to the *National Reformer* in 1874 and later re-published with other poems in 1880.

H. D. Thoreau

I had three chairs in my house; one for solitude, two for friendship, three for society.

Walden: Visitors

The mass of men lead lives of quiet desperation.

Walden: Economy

I never found the companion that was so companionable as solitude.

Walden: Solitude

Love your life, poor as it is. You may perhaps have some pleasant, thrilling, glorious hours, even in a poorhouse.

Walden: Conclusion

Henry David Thoreau (1817-62), the American writer and essayist, was born at Concord, Massachusetts, and educated at Harvard. A mystic, transcendentalist and natural philosopher, he rebelled against the Puritanism of New England and the materialistic values of modern society. He built himself a cabin by Walden Pond and lived there on practically nothing for two-and-a-half years.

Mark Twain

In Boston they ask, How much does he know? In New York, How much is he worth? In Philadelphia, Who were his parents?

What Paul Bourget thinks of us

A classic is something that everybody wants to have read and nobody wants to read.

Speeches: The Disappearance of Literature

Cauliflower is nothing but cabbage with a college education.

Pudd'nhead Wilson's Calendar

They spell it Vinci and pronounce it Vinchy: foreigners always spell better than they pronounce.

The Innocents Abroad

Mark Twain (Samuel Langhorne Clemens, 1835-1910) first came into prominence as a writer with his *Jim Smiley and his Jumping Frog*. His best-known works are *The Innocents Abroad, The Adventures of Tom Sawyer* and *The Adventures of Huckleberry Finn*. He also wrote *A Connecticut Yankee in King Arthur's Court* in 1889.

Virgil

Even here, virtue hath her rewards, and mortality her tears; even here, the woes of man touch the heart of man.

Aeneid

Roman, be this thy care – these thine arts – to bear dominion over the nations and to impose the law of peace, to spare the humbled and to war down the proud.

Aeneid

The last age, heralded in Cumean song, is come, and the great march of the centuries begins anew.

Eclogues

Now the Virgin returns; now Saturn is King again and a new and better race descends from on high.

Eclogues

Virgil (Publius Vergilius Maro, 70-19BC), the Roman poet, was born near Mantua and eulogized his own yeoman class in his poems. His *Eclogues* (ten pastoral poems) appeared in 37BC and were followed in 30BC by the *Georgics*, confirming him as the chief poet of the age. The last years of his life were spent in composing the *Aeneid*, an epic poem in twelve books intended to glorify the Julian dynasty, whose head was Augustus, his own patron. An apparent forecast of the birth of Christ in the fourth *Eclogue* led to his acceptance as an 'honorary' Christian by the medieval Church and in popular legend he became a powerful magician.

Duke of Wellington

I don't know what effect these men will have upon the enemy, but, by God, they terrify me.

On a draft of troops sent to him in Spain, 1809

All the business of war, and indeed all the business of life, is to endeavour to find out what you don't know by what you do; that's what I called 'guessing what was at the other side of the hill'.

Croker Papers

It has been a damned serious business – Blücher and I have lost 30,000 men.

Creevey Papers

It has been a damned nice thing – the nearest run thing you ever saw in your life ... By God! I don't think it would have done if I had not been there.

Creevey Papers

Arthur Wellesley (1769-1852), first Duke of Wellington, was born in Ireland and educated at Eton. He then entered the army and was sent to India. There he achieved victories over the Mahrattas at Assaye and Argaum, and negotiated a Peace which earned him a knighthood. After establishing his reputation in the Peninsular War he defeated the

French at Vimeiro, expelled the French from Spain, and was made Duke of Wellington. Following Napoleon's escape from Elba, he defeated him at Quatre-Bras and at Waterloo.

H. G. Wells

I was thinking jest what a Rum Go everything is.

Kipps

The world may discover that all its common interests are being managed by one concern . . .

A Short History of the World

Herbert George Wells (1866-1946) was the son of a professional cricketer. He took a degree at the Royal College of Science, South Kensington, taught for some years, then made his name in science fiction with such publications as *The Time Machine, The Invisible Man* and *The War of the Worlds*. Later he wrote more stories, including *Kipps, The History of Mr. Polly* and *The Shape of Things to Come*.

John Wesley

Do all the good you can,
By all the means you can,
In all the ways you can,
In all the places you can,
At all the times you can,
To all the people you can,
As long as ever you can.

Methodist Rule of Conduct

John Wesley (1703-91) was the brother of Charles Wesley, the founder of a 'methodist' society of pious young men and composer of many hymns including 'Jesu, lover of my soul'. John Wesley was a man of real and deep learning. He published twenty-three collections of hymns as well as his collected prose *Works*, and his *Journal* which is remarkable for its pathos, humour, and observation of mankind. Methodism was a movement of reaction against the apathy of the Church of England that prevailed in the early part of the eighteenth century.

ACKNOWLEDGEMENTS AND SOURCES

Bournemouth Central Reference Library
Winton (Bournemouth) Library

Concise Oxford Dictionary of English Literature
Concise Oxford Dictionary of Quotations
Everyman's Dictionary of Quotations and Proverbs
Hutchinson's New Twentieth Century Encylopaedia
International Who's Who
New Oxford Book of English Verse 1250–1950
Pears Cyclopaedia
The Book of a Thousand Poems

INDEX OF AUTHORS

Shaw, George Bernard	(1856-1950)	49
Smiles, Samuel	(1812-1904)	50
Smith, Logan Pearsall	(1865-1946)	50
Spenser, Edmund	(1522-92)	51
Staël, Madame de	(1766-1877)	51
Stanhope, Philip Dormer	(1694-1773)	52
Stendhal	(1783-1842)	52
Stevenson, Robert Louis	(1850-94)	53
Tagore, Sir Rabindranath	(1861-1941)	54
Talfourd, Sir Thomas	(1795-1854)	54
Talleyrand, Charles Maurice de	(1754-1838)	54
Tennyson, Alfred, Lord	(1809-92)	55
Thomas, Dylan	(1914-53)	56
Thomson, James	(1834-82)	57
Thoreau, Henry David	(1817-62)	57
Twain, Mark	(1835-1910)	58
Virgil, Publius Vergilius Maro	(70-19BC)	58
Wellesley, Arthur, Duke of Wellington	(1769-1852)	59
Wells, Herbert George	(1866-1946)	60
Wesley, John	(1703-91)	60